Trotskyism or Leninism?

Trotskyism or Leninism?

Joseph Stalin

SAI Press
Dickinson, ND

This edition first published July, 2021.

ISBN: 978-1-300-02865-9

Contents

Introduction

The following was delivered by J.V. Stalin at the Plenum of the Communist Group in the A.U.C.C.T.U., November 19, 1924.

Comrades, after Kamenev's comprehensive report there is little left for me to say. I shall therefore confine myself to exposing certain legends that are being spread by Trotsky and his supporters about the October uprising, about Trotsky's role in the uprising, about the Party and the preparation for October, and so forth. I shall also touch upon Trotskyism as a peculiar ideology that is incompatible with Leninism, and upon the Party's tasks in connection with Trotsky's latest literary pronouncements.

The Facts About The October Uprising

First of all about the October uprising. Rumours are being vigorously spread among members of the Party that the Central Committee as a whole was opposed to an uprising in October 1917. The usual story is that on October 10, when the Central Committee adopted the decision to organise the uprising, the majority of the Central Committee at first spoke against an uprising, but, so the story runs, at that moment a worker burst in on the meeting of the Central Committee and said:

"You are deciding against an uprising, but I tell you that there will be an uprising all the same, in spite of everything." And so, after that threat, the story runs, the Central Committee, which is alleged to have become frightened, raised the question of an uprising afresh and adopted a decision to organise it.

This is not merely a rumour, comrades. It is related by the well-known John Reed in his book *Ten Days*. Reed was remote from our Party and, of course, could not know the history of our secret meeting on October 10, and, consequently, he was taken in by the gossip spread by people like Sukhanov. This story was later passed round and repeated in a number of pamphlets written by Trotskyites, including one of the latest pamphlets on October written by Syrkin. These rumours have been strongly supported in Trotsky's latest literary pronouncements.

It scarcely needs proof that all these and

similar "Arabian Nights" fairy tales are not in accordance with the truth, that in fact nothing of the kind happened, nor could have happened, at the meeting of the Central Committee. Consequently, we could ignore these absurd rumours; after all, lots of rumours are fabricated in the office rooms of the oppositionists or those who are remote from the Party. Indeed, we have ignored them till now; for example, we paid no attention to John Reed's mistakes and did not take the trouble to rectify them. After Trotsky's latest pronouncements, however, it is no longer possible to ignore such legends, for attempts are being made now to bring up our young people on them and, unfortunately, some results have already been achieved in this respect. In view of this, I must counter these absurd rumours with the actual facts.

I take the minutes of the meeting of the

Central Committee of our Party on October 10 (23), 1917. Present Lenin, Zinoviev, Kamenev, Stalin, Trotsky, Sverdlov, Uritsky, Dzerzhinsky, Kollontai, Bubnov, Sokolnikov, Lomov. The question of the current situation and the uprising was discussed. After the discussion, Comrade Lenin's resolution on the uprising was put to the vote. The resolution was adopted by a majority of 10 against 2. Clear, one would think: by a majority of 10 against 2, the Central Committee decided to proceed with the immediate, practical work of organising the uprising. At this very same meeting the Central Committee elected a *political* centre to direct the uprising; this centre, called the Political Bureau, consisted of Lenin, Zinoviev, Stalin, Kamenev, Trotsky, Sokolnikov and Bubnov.

Such are the facts.

These minutes at one stroke destroy several legends. They destroy the legend that the majority on the Central Committee was opposed to an uprising. They also destroy the legend that on the question of the uprising the Central Committee was on the verge of a split. It is clear from the minutes that the opponents of an immediate uprising -- Kamenev and Zinoviev -- were elected to the body that was to exercise political direction of the uprising on a par with those who were in favour of an uprising. There was no question of a split, nor could there be.

Trotsky asserts that in October our Party had a Right wing in the persons of Kamenev and Zinoviev, who, he says, were almost Social-Democrats. What one cannot understand then is how, under those circumstances, it could happen that the Party avoided a split; how it could happen that the disagreements with Kamenev and Zinoviev lasted only a few days; how it could happen that, in spite of those disagreements, the Party appointed these comrades to highly important posts, elected them to the political centre of the uprising, and so forth. Lenin's implacable attitude towards Social-Democrats is sufficiently well-known in the Party; the Party knows that Lenin would not for a single moment have agreed to have Social-Democratically-minded comrades in the Party, let alone in highly important posts. How, then, are we to explain the fact that the Party avoided a split? The explanation is that in spite of the disagreements, these comrades were old Bolsheviks who stood on the common ground of Bolshevism. What was that common ground? Unity of views on the fundamental questions: the character of the Russian revolution, the driving forces of the revolution, the role of the peasantry, the principles of Party leadership, and so forth. Had there not been this common ground, a split would have been inevitable. There was no split, and the disagreements lasted only a few days, because, and only because, Kamenev and Zinoviev were Leninists, Bolsheviks.

Let us now pass to the legend about Trotsky's special role in the October uprising. The Trotskyites are vigorously spreading rumours that Trotsky inspired and was the sole leader of the October uprising. These rumours are being spread with exceptional zeal by the so-called editor of Trotsky's works, Lentsner. Trotsky himself, by consistently avoiding mention of the Party, the Central Committee and the Petrograd Committee of the Party, by saying nothing about the leading role of these organisation, in the uprising and vigorously pushing himself forward as the central figure in the October uprising, voluntarily or involuntarily helps to spread the rumours about the special role he is supposed to have played in the uprising. I am far from denying Trotsky's undoubtedly important role in the uprising. I must say, however, that Trotsky did not play any special role in the October uprising, nor could he do so; being chairman of the Petrograd Soviet, he merely carried out the will of the appropriate Party bodies, which directed every step that Trotsky took. To philistines like Sukhanov, all this may seem strange, but the facts, the true facts, wholly and fully confirm what I say.

Let us take the minutes of the next meeting of the Central Committee, the one held on October 16 (29), 1917. Present: the members of the Central Committee, plus representatives of the Petrograd Committee, plus representatives of the military organisation, factory committees, trade unions and the railwaymen. Among those present, besides the members of the Central Committee, were: Krylenko, Shotman, Kalinin, Volodarsky, Shlyapnikov, Lacis, and others, twenty-five in all. The question of the uprising was discussed from the purely practical-organisational aspect. Lenin's resolution on the uprising was adopted by a majority of 20 against 2, three abstaining. A *practical* centre was elected for the organisational leadership of the uprising. Who was elected to this centre? The following five: Sverdlov, Stalin, Dzerzhinsky, Bubnov, Uritsky. The functions of the practical centre: to direct all the practical organs of the uprising in conformity with the directives of the Central Committee. Thus, as you see, something "terrible" happened at this meeting of the Central Committee, i.e., "strange to relate," the "inspirer," the "chief figure," the "sole leader" of the uprising, Trotsky, was not elected to the practical centre, which was called upon to direct the uprising. How is this to be reconciled with the current opinion about Trotsky's special role? Is not all this somewhat "strange," as Sukhanov, or the Trotskyites, would say? And yet, strictly speaking, there is nothing strange about it, for neither in the Party, nor in the October uprising, did Trotsky play any *special* role, nor could he do so, for he was a relatively new man in our Party in the period of October. He, like all the responsible workers, merely carried out the will of the Central Committee and of its organs. Whoever is familiar with the mechanics of Bolshevik Party leadership will have no difficulty in understanding that it could not be otherwise: it would have been enough for Trotsky to have gone against the will of the Central Committee to have been deprived of influence on the course of events. This talk about Trotsky's special role is a legend that is being spread by obliging "Party" gossips.

This, of course, does not mean that the October uprising did not have its inspirer. It did have its inspirer and leader, but this was Lenin, and none other than Lenin, that same Lenin whose resolutions the Central Committee adopted when deciding the question of the uprising, that same Lenin who, in spite of what Trotsky says, was not prevented by being in hiding from being the actual inspirer of the uprising. It is foolish and ridiculous to attempt now, by gossip about Lenin having been in hiding, to obscure the indubitable fact that the inspirer of the uprising was the leader of the

Party, V. I. Lenin.

Such are the facts.

Granted, we are told, but it cannot be denied that Trotsky fought well in the period of October. Yes, that is true, Trotsky did, indeed, fight well in October; but Trotsky was not the only one who fought well in the period of October. Even people like the Left Socialist-Revolutionaries, who then stood side by side with the Bolsheviks, also fought well. In general, I must say that in the period of a victorious uprising, when the enemy is isolated and the uprising is growing, it is not difficult to fight well. At such moments even backward people become heroes.

The proletarian struggle is not, however, an uninterrupted advance, an unbroken chain of victories. The proletarian struggle also has its trials, its defeats. The genuine revolutionary is not one who displays courage in the period of a victorious uprising, but one who, while fighting well during the victorious advance of the revolution, also displays courage when the revolution is in retreat, when the proletariat suffers defeat; who does not lose his head and does not funk when the revolution suffers reverses, when the enemy achieves success; who does not become panic-stricken or give way to despair when the revolution is in a period of retreat. The Left Socialist-Revolutionaries did not fight badly in the period of October, and they supported the Bolsheviks. But who does not know that those "brave" fighters became panic-stricken in the period of Brest, when the advance of German imperialism drove them to despair and hysteria. It is a very sad but indubitable fact that Trotsky, who fought well in the period of October, did not, in the period of Brest, in the period when the revolution suffered temporary reverses, possess the courage to display sufficient staunchness at that difficult moment and to refrain from following in the footsteps of the Left Socialist-Revolutionaries. Beyond question, that moment was a difficult one; one had to display exceptional courage and imperturbable coolness not to be dismayed, to retreat in good time, to accept peace in good time, to withdraw the proletarian army out of range of the blows of German imperialism, to preserve the peasant reserves and, after obtaining a respite in this way, to strike at the enemy with renewed force. Unfortunately, Trotsky was found to lack this courage and revolutionary staunchness at that difficult moment.

In Trotsky's opinion, the principal lesson

of the proletarian revolution is "not to funk" during October. That is wrong, for Trotsky's assertion contains only a *particle* of the truth about the lessons of the revolution. The *whole* truth about the lessons of the proletarian revolution is "not to funk" not only when the revolution is advancing, but also when it is in retreat, when the enemy is gaining the upper hand and the revolution is suffering reverses. The revolution did not end with October. October was only the beginning of the proletarian revolution. It is bad to funk when the tide of insurrection is rising; but it is worse to funk when the revolution is passing through severe trials after power has been captured. To retain power on the morrow of the revolution is no less important than to capture power. If Trotsky funked during the period of Brest, when our revolution was passing through severe trials, when it was almost a matter of "surrendering" power, he ought to know that the mistakes committed by Kamenev and Zinoviev in October are quite irrelevant here.

That is how matters stand with the legends about the October uprising.

The Party And The Preperation For October

Let us now pass to the question of the preparation for October.

Listening to Trotsky, one might think that during the whole of the period of preparation, from March to October, the Bolshevik Party did nothing but mark time; that it was being corroded by internal contradictions and hindered Lenin in every way; that, had it not been for Trotsky, nobody knows how the October Revolution would have ended. It is rather amusing to hear this strange talk about the Party from Trotsky, who declares in this same "preface" to Volume III that "the chief instrument of the proletarian revolution is the Party," that "without the Party, apart from the Party, by-passing the Party, with a substitute for the Party, the proletarian revolution cannot be victorious." Allah himself would not understand how our revolution could have succeeded if "its chief instrument" proved to be useless, while success was impossible, as it appears, "by-passing the Party." But this is not the first time that Trotsky treats us to oddities. It must be supposed that this amusing talk about our Party is one of Trotsky's usual oddities.

Let us briefly review the history of the preparation for October according to periods.

1) *The period of the Party's new orientation (March-April).* The major facts of this period:

a) the overthrow of tsarism;

25

b) the formation of the Provisional Government (dictatorship of the bourgeoisie);

c) the appearance of Soviets of Workers' and Soldiers' Deputies (dictatorship of the proletariat and peasantry);

d) dual power;

e) the April demonstration;

f) the first crisis of power.

The characteristic feature of this period is the fact that there existed together, side by side and simultaneously, both the dictatorship of the bourgeoisie and the dictatorship of the proletariat and peasantry; the latter trusts the former, believes that it is striving for peace, voluntarily surrenders power to the bourgeoisie and thereby becomes an appendage of the bourgeoisie. There are as yet no serious conflicts between the two dictatorships. On the other hand, there is the "Contact Committee."

This was the greatest turning point in the history of Russia and an unprecedented turning point in the history of our Party. The old, pre-revolutionary platform of direct overthrow of the government was clear and definite, but it was no longer suitable for the new conditions of the struggle. It was now no longer possible to go straight out for the overthrow of the government, for the latter was connected with the Soviets, then under the influence of the defencists, and the Party would have had to wage war against both the government and the Soviets, a war that would have been beyond its strength. Nor was it possible to pursue a policy of supporting the Provisional Government, for it was the government of imperialism. Under the new conditions of the struggle, the Party had to adopt a new orientation. The Party (its majority) groped its way towards this new orientation. It adopted the policy of pressure on the Provisional Government through the Soviets on the question of peace and did not venture to step forward at once from the old slogan of the dictatorship of the proletariat and peasantry to the new slogan of power to the Soviets. The aim of this halfway policy was to enable the Soviets to discern the actual imperialist nature of the Provisional Government on the basis of the concrete questions of peace, and in this way to wrest the Soviets from the Provisional Government. But this was a profoundly mistaken position, for it gave rise to pacifist illusions, brought grist to the mill of defencism and hindered the revolutionary education of the masses. At that time I shared this mistaken position with other Party comrades and fully abandoned it only in the middle of April, when I associated myself with Lenin's theses. A new orientation was needed. This new orientation was given to the Party by Lenin, in his celebrated April Theses. I shall not deal with these theses, for they are known to everybody. Were there any disagreements between the Party and Lenin at that time? Yes, there were. How long did these disagreements last? Not more than two weeks. The City Conference of the Petrograd organisation (in the latter half of April), which adopted Lenin's theses, marked a turning point in our Party's development. The All-Russian April Conference (at the end of April) merely completed on an all-Russian scale the work of the Petrograd Conference, rallying nine-tenths of the Party around this united Party position.

Now, seven years later, Trotsky gloats

maliciously over the past disagreements among the Bolsheviks and depicts them as a struggle waged as if there were almost two parties within Bolshevism. But, firstly, Trotsky disgracefully exaggerates and inflates the matter, for the Bolshevik Party lived through these disagreements without the slightest shock. Secondly, our Party would be a caste and not a revolutionary party if it did not permit different shades of opinion in its ranks. Moreover, it is well known that there were disagreements among us even before that, for example, in the period of the Third Duma, but they did not shake the unity of our Party. Thirdly, it will not be out of place to ask what was *then* the position of Trotsky himself, who is *now* gloating so eagerly over the past disagreements among the Bolsheviks. Lentsner, the so-called editor of Trotsky's works, assures us that Trotsky's letters from America (March) "wholly anticipated" Lenin's *Letters From Afar* (March), which served as the basis of Lenin's April Theses. That is what he says: "wholly anticipated." Trotsky does not object to this analogy; apparently, he accepts it with thanks. But, firstly, Trotsky's letters "do not in the least resemble" Lenin's letters either in spirit or in conclusions, for they wholly and entirely reflect Trotsky's anti-Bolshevik slogan of "no tsar, but a workers' government," a slogan which implies a revolution *without* the peasantry. It is enough to glance through these two series of letters to be convinced of this. Secondly, if what Lentener says is true, how are we to explain the fact that Lenin on the very next day after his arrival from abroad considered it necessary to dissociate himself from Trotsky? Who does not know of Lenin's repeated statements that Trotsky's slogan: "*no tsar, but a workers' government*" was an attempt "to skip the still unexhausted peasant movement," that this slogan meant "playing at the seizure of power by a workers' government"?

What can there be in common between Lenin's Bolshevik theses and Trotsky's anti-Bolshevik scheme with its "playing at the seizure of power"? And what prompts this passion that some people display for comparing a wretched hovel with Mont Blanc? For what purpose did Lentsner find it necessary to make this risky addition to the heap of old legends about our revolution of still another legend, about Trotsky's letters from America "anticipating" Lenin's well-known *Letters From Afar*?

No wonder it is said that an obliging fool

is more dangerous than an enemy.

2) *The period of the revolutionary mobilisation of the masses (May-August).* The major facts of this period:

a) the April demonstration in Petrograd and the formation of the coalition government with the participation of "Socialists";

b) the May Day demonstrations in the principal centres of Russia with the slogan of "a democratic peace";

c) the June demonstration in Petrograd with the principal slogan: "Down with the capitalist ministers!";

d) the June offensive at the front and the reverses of the Russian army;

e) the July armed demonstration in Petrograd; the Cadet ministers resign from the government;

f) counter-revolutionary troops are called in from the front; the editorial offices of *Pravda* are wrecked; the counter-revolution launches a struggle against the Soviets and a new coalition government is formed, headed by Kerensky;

g) the Sixth Congress of our Party, which issues the slogan to prepare for an armed uprising;

h) the counter-revolutionary Conference of State and the general strike in Moscow;

i) Kornilov's unsuccessful march on Petrograd, the revitalising of the Soviets; the Cadets resign and a "Directory" is formed.

The characteristic feature of this period is the intensification of the crisis and the upsetting of the unstable equilibrium between the Soviets and the Provisional Government which, for good or evil, had existed in the preceding period. Dual power has become intolerable for both sides. The fragile edifice of the "Contact Committee" is tottering. "Crisis of power" and "ministerial re-shuffle" are the most fashionable catchwords of the day. The crisis at the front and the disruption in the rear are doing their work, strengthening the extreme flanks and squeezing the defencist compromisers from both sides. The revolution is mobilising, causing the mobilisation of the counter-revolution. The counter-revolution, in its turn, is spurring on the revolution, stirring up new waves of the revolutionary tide. The question of transferring power to the new class becomes the immediate question of the day.

Were there disagreements in our Party then? Yes, there were. They were, however, of a purely practical character, despite the assertions of Trotsky, who is trying to discover a "Right" and a "Left" wing in the Party. That is to say, they were such disagreements as are inevitable where there is vigorous Party life and real Party activity.

Trotsky is wrong in asserting that the April demonstration in Petrograd gave rise to disagreements in the Central Committee. The Central Committee was absolutely united on this question and condemned the attempt of a group of comrades to arrest the Provisional Government at a time when the Bolsheviks were in a minority both in the Soviets and in the army. Had Trotsky written the "history" of October not according to Sukhanov, but according to authentic documents, he would easily have convinced himself of the error of his assertion.

Trotsky is absolutely wrong in asserting that the attempt, "on Lenin's initiative," to arrange a demonstration on June 10 was described as "adventurism" by the "Rightwing" members of the Central Committee. Had Trotsky not written according to Sukhanov he would surely have known that the June 10 demonstration was postponed with the full agreement of Lenin, and that he urged the necessity of postponing it in a big speech he delivered at the well-known meeting of the Petrograd Committee (see minutes of the Petrograd Committee).

Trotsky is absolutely wrong in speaking about "tragic" disagreements in the Central Committee in connection with the July armed demonstration. Trotsky is simply inventing in asserting that some members of the leading group in the Central. Committee "could not but

regard the July episode as a harmful adventure."
Trotsky, who was then not yet a member of our
Central Committee and was merely our Soviet
parliamentary, might, of course, not have known
that the Central Committee regarded the July
demonstration only as a means of sounding the
enemy, that the Central Committee (and Lenin)
did not want to convert, did not even think of
converting, the demonstration into an uprising at
a time when the Soviets in the capitals still
supported the defencists. It is quite possible that
some Bolsheviks did whimper over the July
defeat. I know, for example, that some of the
Bolsheviks who were arrested at the time were
even prepared to desert our ranks. But to draw
inferences from this against certain alleged
"Rights," alleged to be members of the Central
Committee, is a shameful distortion of history.

Trotsky is wrong in declaring that during

the Kornilov days a section of the Party leaders inclined towards the formation of a bloc with the defencists, towards supporting the Provisional Government. He, of course, is referring to those same alleged "Rights" who keep him awake at night. Trotsky is wrong, for there exist documents, such as the Central Organ of the Party of that time, which refute his statements. Trotsky refers to Lenin's letter to the Central Committee warning against supporting Kerensky; but Trotsky fails to understand Lenin's letters, their significance, their purpose. In his letters, Lenin sometimes deliberately ran ahead, pushing into the forefront mistakes that might *possibly* be committed, and criticising them in advance with the object of warning the Party and of safeguarding it against mistakes. Sometimes he would even magnify a "trifle" and "make a mountain out of a molehill" for the same pedagogical purpose. The leader of the party, especially if he is in hiding, cannot act otherwise, for he must see further than his comrades-in-arms, he must sound the alarm over every possible mistake, even over "trifles." But to infer from such letters of Lenin's (and he wrote quite a number of such letters) the existence of "tragic" disagreements and to trumpet them forth means not to understand Lenin's letters, means not to know Lenin. This, probably, explains why Trotsky sometimes is wide of the mark. In short: there were no disagreements in the Central Committee during the Kornilov revolt, absolutely none.

After the July defeat, disagreement did indeed arise between the Central Committee and Lenin on the question of the future of the Soviets. It is known that Lenin, wishing to concentrate the Party's attention on the task of preparing the uprising outside the Soviets, warned against any infatuation with the latter, for he was of the opinion that, having been defiled by the defencists, they had become useless. The Central Committee and the Sixth Party Congress took a more cautious line and decided that there were no grounds for excluding the possibility that the Soviets would revive. The Kornilov revolt showed that this decision was correct. This disagreement, however, was of no great consequence for the Party. Later, Lenin admitted that the line taken by the Sixth Congress had been correct. It is interesting that Trotsky has not clutched at this disagreement and has not magnified it to "monstrous" proportions.

A united and solid party, the hub of the revolutionary mobilisation of the masses -- such was the picture presented by our Party in that period.

3) *The period of organisation of the assault (September-October).* The major facts of this period:

a) the convocation of the Democratic Conference and the collapse of the idea of a bloc with the Cadets;

b) the Moscow and Petrograd Soviets go over to the side of the Bolsheviks;

c) the Congress of Soviets of the Northern Region; the Petrograd Soviet decides against the withdrawal of the troops;

d) the decision of the Central Committee on the uprising and the formation of the Revolutionary Military Committee of the Petrograd Soviet;

e) the Petrograd garrison decides to

render the Petrograd Soviet armed support; a network of commissars of the Revolutionary Military Committee is organised;

f) the Bolshevik armed forces go into action; the members of the Provisional Government are arrested;

g) the Revolutionary Military Committee of the Petrograd Soviet takes power; the Second Congress of Soviets sets up the Council of People's Commissars.

The characteristic feature of this period is the rapid growth of the crisis, the utter consternation reigning among the ruling circles, the isolation of the Socialist-Revolutionaries and Mensheviks, and the mass flight of the vacillating elements to the side of the Bolsheviks. A peculiar feature of the tactics of the revolution in this period must be noted, namely, that the revolution strove to take every, or nearly every, step in its attack in the guise of defence. Undoubtedly, the refusal to allow the troops to be withdrawn from Petrograd was an important step in the revolution's attack; nevertheless, this attack was carried out under the slogan of protecting Petrograd from possible attack by the external enemy. Undoubtedly, the formation of the Revolutionary Military Committee was a still more important step in the attack upon the Provisional Government; nevertheless, it was carried out under the slogan of organising Soviet control over the actions of the Headquarters of the Military Area. Undoubtedly, the open transition of the garrison to the side of the Revolutionary Military Committee and the organisation of a network of Soviet Commissars marked the beginning of the uprising; nevertheless, the revolution took these steps under the slogan of protecting the Petrograd Soviet from possible action by the counterrevolution. The revolution, as it were, masked its actions in attack under the cloak of defence in order the more easily to draw the irresolute, vacillating elements into its orbit. This, no doubt, explains the outwardly defensive character of the speeches, articles and slogans of that period, the inner content of which, none the less, was of a profoundly attacking nature.

Were there disagreements in the Central Committee in that period? Yes, there were, and fairly important ones at that. I have already spoken about the disagreements over the uprising. They are fully reflected in the minutes of the meetings of the Central Committee of October 10 and 16. I shall, therefore, not repeat what I have already said. Three questions must now be dealt with: participation in the Pre-parliament, the role of the Soviets in the uprising, and the date of the uprising. This is all the more necessary because Trotsky, in his zeal to push himself into a prominent place, has "inadvertently" misrepresented the stand Lenin took on the last two questions.

Undoubtedly, the disagreements on the question of the Pre-parliament were of a serious nature. What was, so to speak, the aim of the Pre-parliament? It was: to help the bourgeoisie to push the Soviets into the background and to lay the foundations of bourgeois parliamentarism. Whether the Pre-parliament could have accomplished this task in the revolutionary situation that had arisen is another matter. Events showed that this aim could not be realised, and the Pre-parliament itself was a Kornilovite abortion. There can be no doubt, however, that it was precisely this aim that the

Mensheviks and Socialist-Revolutionaries pursued in setting up the Pre-parliament. What could the Bolsheviks' participation in the Pre-parliament mean under those circumstances? Nothing but deceiving the proletarian masses about the true nature of the Pre-parliament. This is the chief explanation for the passion with which Lenin, in his letters, scourged those who were in favour of taking part in the Pre-parliament. There can be no doubt that it was a grave mistake to have taken part in the Pre-parliament.

It would be a mistake, however, to think, as Trotsky does, that those who were in favour of taking part in the Pre-parliament went into it for the purpose of constructive work, for the purpose of "directing the working-class movement" "into the channel of Social-Democracy." That is not at all the case. It is not true. Had that been the case, the Party would not have been able to rectify this mistake "in two ticks" by demonstratively walking out of the Pre-parliament. Incidentally, the swift rectification of this mistake was an expression of our Party's vitality and revolutionary might.

And now, permit me to correct a slight inaccuracy that has crept into the report of Lentsner, the "editor" of Trotsky's works, about the meeting of the Bolshevik group at which a decision on the question of the Pre-parliament was taken. Lentsner says that there were two reporters at this meeting, Kamenev and Trotsky. That is not true. Actually, there were four reporters: two in favour of boycotting the Pre-parliament (Trotsky and Stalin), and two in favour of participation (Kamenev and Nogin).

Trotsky is in a still worse position when

dealing with the stand Lenin took on the question of the form of the uprising. According to Trotsky, it appears that Lenin's view was that the Party should take power in October "independently of and behind the back of the Soviet." Later on, criticising this nonsense, which he ascribes to Lenin, Trotsky "cuts capers" and finally delivers the following condescending utterance:

"That would have been a mistake." Trotsky is here uttering a falsehood about Lenin, he is misrepresenting Lenin's views on the role of the Soviets in the uprising. A pile of documents can be cited, showing that Lenin proposed that power be taken *through* the Soviets, either the Petrograd or the Moscow Soviet, and not *behind the back* of the Soviets. Why did Trotsky have to invent this more than strange legend about Lenin?

Nor is Trotsky in a better position when he "analyses" the stand taken by the Central Committee and Lenin on the question of the date of the uprising. Reporting the famous meeting of the Central Committee of October 10, Trotsky asserts that at that meeting "a resolution was carried to the effect that the uprising should take place not later than October 15." From this it appears that the Central Committee fixed October 15 as the date of the uprising and then itself violated that decision by postponing the date of the uprising to October 25. Is that true? No, it is not. During that period the Central Committee passed only two resolutions on the uprising -- one on October 10 and the other on October 16. Let us read these resolutions.

The Central Committee's resolution of October 10:

"The Central Committee recognises that the international position of the Russian revolution (the mutiny in the German navy, which is an extreme manifestation of the growth throughout Europe of the world socialist revolution, and the threat of peace between the imperialists with the object of strangling the revolution in Russia) as well as the military situation (the indubitable decision of the Russian bourgeoisie and Kerensky and Co. to surrender Petrograd to the Germans), and the fact that the proletarian party has gained a majority in the Soviets -- all this, taken in conjunction with the peasant revolt and the swing of popular confidence towards our Party (the elections in Moscow), and, finally, the obvious preparations being made for a second Kornilov affair (the withdrawal of troops from Petrograd, the dispatch of Cossacks to

Petrograd, the surrounding of Minsk by Cossacks, etc.) -- all this places an armed uprising on the order of the day.

"Considering, therefore, that an armed uprising is inevitable, and that the time for it is fully ripe, the Central Committee instructs all Party organisations to be guided accordingly, and to discuss and decide all practical questions (the Congress of Soviets of the Northern Region, the withdrawal of troops from Petrograd, the actions of the people in Moscow and Minsk, etc.) from this point of view."

The resolution adopted by the conference of the Central Committee with responsible workers on October 16:

"This meeting fully welcomes and wholly supports the Central Committee's resolution, calls upon all organisations and all workers and soldiers to make thorough and most intense preparations for an armed uprising and for support of the centre set up by the Central Committee for this purpose, and expresses complete confidence that the Central Committee and the Soviet will in good time indicate the favourable moment and the suitable means for launching the attack."

You see that Trotsky's memory betrayed him about the date of the uprising and the Central Committee's resolution on the uprising.

Trotsky is absolutely wrong in asserting that Lenin underrated Soviet legality, that Lenin failed to appreciate the great importance of the All-Russian Congress of Soviets taking power on October 25, and that this was the reason why he insisted that power be taken before October 25. That is not true. Lenin proposed that power be taken before October 25 for two reasons. Firstly, because the counter-revolutionaries might have surrendered Petrograd at any moment, which would have drained the blood of the developing uprising, and so every day was precious. Secondly, because the mistake made by the Petrograd Soviet in *openly* fixing and announcing the day of the uprising (October 25) could not be rectified in any other way than by actually launching the uprising *before* the legal date set for it. The fact of the matter is that Lenin regarded insurrection as an art, and he could not help knowing that the enemy, informed about the date of the uprising (owing to the carelessness of the Petrograd Soviet) would certainly try to prepare for that day. Consequently, it was necessary to forestall the enemy, i.e., without fail to launch the uprising *before* the legal date. This is the chief explanation for the passion with which Lenin in his letters scourged those who made a fetish of the date -- October 25. Events showed that Lenin was absolutely right. It is well known that the uprising was launched prior to the All-Russian Congress of Soviets. It is well known that power was actually taken before the opening of the All-Russian Congress of Soviets, and it was taken not by the Congress of Soviets, but by the Petrograd Soviet, by the Revolutionary Military Committee. The Congress of Soviets merely *took over* power from the Petrograd Soviet. That is why Trotsky's lengthy arguments about the importance of Soviet legality are quite beside the point.

A virile and mighty party standing at the head of the revolutionary masses who were storming and overthrowing bourgeois rule -- such was the state of our Party in that period.

That is how matters stand with the legends about the preparation for October.

Trotskyism or Leninism?

We have dealt above with the legends directed against the Party and those about Lenin spread by Trotsky and his supporters in connection with October and the preparation for it. We have exposed and refuted these legends. But the question arises: For what purpose did Trotsky need all these legends about October and the preparation for October, about Lenin and the Party of Lenin? What is the purpose of Trotsky's new literary pronouncements against the Party? What is the sense, the purpose, the aim of these pronouncements now, when the Party does not want a discussion, when the Party is busy with a host of urgent tasks, when the Party needs united efforts to restore our economy and not a new struggle around old questions? For what purpose does Trotsky need to drag the Party back, to new discussions?

Trotsky asserts that all this is needed for the purpose of "studying" October. But is it not possible to study October without giving another kick at the Party and its leader Lenin? What sort of a "history" of October is it that begins and ends with attempts to discredit the chief leader of the October uprising, to discredit the Party, which organised and carried through the uprising? No, it is not a matter here of studying October. *That is* not the way to study October. *That is* not the way to write the history of October. Obviously, there is a different "design" here, and everything goes to show that this "design" is that Trotsky by his literary pronouncements is making another (yet another!) attempt to create the conditions for substituting Trotskyism for Leninism. Trotsky needs "desperately" to discredit the Party, and its cadres who carried through the uprising, in order, after discrediting the Party, to proceed to discredit Leninism. And it is necessary for him to discredit Leninism in order to drag in Trotskyism as the "sole" "proletarian" (don't laugh!) ideology. All this, of course (oh, of course!) under the flag of Leninism, so that the dragging operation may be performed "as painlessly as possible. "

That is the essence of Trotsky's latest literary pronouncements.

That is why those literary pronouncements of Trotsky's sharply raise the question of Trotskyism.

And so, what is Trotskyism?

Trotskyism possesses three specific features which bring it into irreconcilable contradiction with Leninism.

What are these features?

Firstly. Trotskyism is the theory of "permanent" (uninterrupted) revolution. But what is permanent revolution in its Trotskyist interpretation? It is revolution that fails to take the poor peasantry into account as a revolutionary force. Trotsky's "permanent" revolution is, as Lenin said, "skipping" the peasant movement, "playing at the seizure of power." Why is it dangerous? Because such a revolution, if an attempt had been made to bring it about, would inevitably have ended in failure, for it would have divorced from the Russian proletariat its ally, the poor peasantry. This explains the struggle that Leninism has been waging against Trotskyism ever since 1905.

How does Trotsky appraise Leninism from the standpoint of this struggle? He regards it as a theory that possesses "anti-revolutionary features." What is this indignant opinion about Leninism based on? On the fact that, at the proper time, Leninism advocated and upheld the idea of the dictatorship of the proletariat and *peasantry*.

But Trotsky does not confine himself to this indignant opinion. He goes further and asserts: "The entire edifice of Leninism at the present time is built on lies and falsification and bears within itself the poisonous elements of its own decay" (see Trotsky's letter to Chkheidze, 1913). As you see, we have before us two opposite lines.

Secondly. Trotskyism is distrust of the

Bolshevik Party principle, of the monolithic character of the Party, of its hostility towards opportunist elements. In the sphere of organisation, Trotskyism is the theory that revolutionaries and opportunists can co-exist and form groups and coteries within a single party. You are, no doubt, familiar with the history of Trotsky's August bloc, in which the Martovites and Otzovists, the Liquidators and Trotskyites, happily co-operated, pretending that they were a "real" party. It is well known that this patchwork "party" pursued the aim of destroying the Bolshevik Party. What was the nature of "our disagreements" at that time? It was that Leninism regarded the destruction of the August bloc as a guarantee of the development of the proletarian party, whereas Trotskyism regarded that bloc as the basis for building a "real" party.

Again, as you see, we have two opposite lines.

Thirdly. Trotskyism is distrust of the leaders of Bolshevism, an attempt to discredit, to defame them. I do not know of a single trend in the Party that could compare with Trotskyism in the matter of discrediting the leaders of Leninism or the central institutions of the Party. For example, what should be said of Trotsky's "polite" opinion of Lenin, whom he described as "a professional exploiter of every kind of backwardness in the Russian working-class movement"? (*ibid.*) And this is far from being the most "polite" of the "polite" opinions Trotsky has expressed.

How could it happen that Trotsky, who carried such a nasty stock-in-trade on his back, found himself, after all, in the ranks of the

Bolsheviks during the October movement? It happened because at that time Trotsky abandoned (actually did abandon) that stock-in-trade; he hid it in the cupboard. Had he not performed that "operation," real co-operation with him would have been impossible. The theory of the August bloc, i.e., the theory of unity with the Mensheviks, had already been shattered and thrown overboard by the revolution, for how could there be any talk about unity when an armed struggle was raging between the Bolsheviks and the Mensheviks? Trotsky had no alternative but to admit that this theory was useless.

The same misadventure "happened" to the theory of permanent revolution, for not a single Bolshevik contemplated the immediate seizure of power on the morrow of the February Revolution, and Trotsky could not help knowing that the Bolsheviks would not allow him, in the words of Lenin, "to play at the seizure of power." Trotsky had no alternative but recognise the Bolsheviks' policy of fighting for influence in the Soviets, of fighting to win over the peasantry. As regards the third specific feature of Trotskyism (distrust of the Bolshevik leaders), it naturally had to retire into the background owing to the obvious failure of the first two features.

Under those circumstances, could Trotsky do anything else but hide his stock-in-trade in the cupboard and follow the Bolsheviks, considering that he had no group of his own of any significance, and that he came to the Bolsheviks as a political individual, without an army? Of course, he could not!

What is the lesson to be learnt from this?

Only one: that prolonged collaboration between the Leninists and Trotsky is possible only if the latter completely abandons his old stock-in-trade, only if he completely accepts Leninism. Trotsky writes about the lessons of October, but he forgets that, in addition to all the other lessons, there is one more lesson of October, the one I have just mentioned, which is of prime importance for Trotskyism. Trotskyism ought to learn that lesson of October too.

It is evident, however, that Trotskyism has not learnt that lesson. The fact of the matter is that the old stock-in-trade of Trotskyism that was hidden in the cupboard in the period of the October movement is now being dragged into the light again in the hope that a market will be found for it, seeing that the market in our country is expanding. Undoubtedly, Trotsky's new literary pronouncements are an attempt to revert to Trotskyism, to "overcome" Leninism, to drag in, implant, all the specific features of Trotskyism. The new Trotskyism is not a mere repetition of the old Trotskyism; its feathers have been plucked and it is rather bedraggled; it is incomparably milder in spirit and more moderate in form than the old Trotskyism; but, in essence, it undoubtedly retains all the specific features of the old Trotskyism. The new Trotskyism does not dare to come out as a militant force against Leninism; it prefers to operate under the common flag of Leninism, under the slogan of interpreting, improving Leninism. That is because it is weak. It cannot be regarded as an accident that the appearance of the new Trotskyism coincided with Lenin's departure. In Lenin's lifetime it would not have dared to take this risky step.

What are the characteristic features of

the new Trotskyism?

1) ***On the question of "permanent" revolution.*** The new Trotskyism does not deem it necessary openly to uphold the theory of "permanent" revolution. It "simply" asserts that the October Revolution fully confirmed the idea of "permanent" revolution. From this it draws the following conclusion: the important and acceptable part of Leninism is the part that came after the war, in the period of the October Revolution; on the other hand, the part of Leninism that existed before the war, before the October Revolution, is wrong and unacceptable. Hence, the Trotskyites' theory of the division of Leninism into two parts: pre-war Leninism, the "old," "useless" Leninism with its idea of the dictatorship of the proletariat and peasantry, and the new, post-war, October Leninism, which they count on adapting to the requirements of

Trotskyism. Trotskyism needs this theory of the division of Leninism as a first, more or less "acceptable" step that is necessary to facilitate further steps in its struggle against Leninism.

But Leninism is not an eclectic theory stuck together out of diverse elements and capable of being cut into parts. Leninism is an integral theory, which arose in 1903, has passed the test of three revolutions, and is now being carried forward as the battle-flag of the world proletariat.

"Bolshevism," Lenin said, "as a trend of political thought and as a political party, has existed since 1903. Only the history of Bolshevism during the *whole* period of its existence can satisfactorily explain why it was able to build up and to maintain under most difficult conditions the iron discipline needed for the victory of the proletariat" (see Vol. XXV, p. 174).

Bolshevism and Leninism are one. They are two names for one and the same thing. Hence, the theory of the division of Leninism into two parts is a theory intended to destroy Leninism, to substitute Trotskyism for Leninism.

Needless to say, the Party cannot reconcile itself to this grotesque theory.

2) *On the question of the Party principle.* The old Trotskyism tried to undermine the Bolshevik Party principle by means of the theory (and practice) of unity with the Mensheviks. But that theory has suffered such disgrace that nobody now even wants to mention it. To undermine the Party principle, present-day Trotskyism has invented the new, less odious and almost "democratic" theory of contrasting the old cadres to the younger Party element. According to Trotskyism, our Party has not a single and integral history. Trotskyism divides the history of our Party into two parts of unequal importance: pre-October and post-October. The pre-October part of the history of our Party is, properly speaking, not history, but "pre-history," the unimportant or, at all events, not very important preparatory period of our Party. The post-October part of the history of our Party, however, is real, genuine history. In the former, there are the "old," "pre-historic," unimportant cadres of our Party. In the latter there is the new, real, "historic" Party. It scarcely needs proof that this singular scheme of the history of the Party is a scheme to disrupt the unity between the old and the new cadres of our Party, a scheme to destroy the Bolshevik Party

71

principle.

Needless to say, the Party cannot reconcile itself to this grotesque scheme.

3) *On the question of the leaders of Bolshevism.* The old Trotskyism tried to discredit Lenin more or less openly, without fearing the consequences. The new Trotskyism is more cautious. It tries to achieve the purpose of the old Trotskyism by pretending to praise, to exalt Lenin. I think it is worth while quoting a few examples.

The Party knows that Lenin was a relentless revolutionary; but it knows also that he was cautious, that he disliked reckless people and often, with a firm hand, restrained those who were infatuated with terrorism, including Trotsky himself. Trotsky touches on this subject in his book *On Lenin*, but from his portrayal of

Lenin one might think that all Lenin did was "at every opportunity to din into people's minds the idea that terrorism was inevitable." The impression is created that Lenin was the most bloodthirsty of all the bloodthirsty Bolsheviks.

For what purpose did Trotsky need this uncalled for and totally unjustified exaggeration?

The Party knows that Lenin was an exemplary Party man, who did not like to settle questions alone, without the leading collective body, on the spur of the moment, without careful investigation and verification. Trotsky touches upon this aspect, too, in his book. But the portrait he paints is not that of Lenin, but of a sort of Chinese mandarin, who settles important questions in the quiet of his study, by intuition.

Do you want to know how our Party settled the question of dispersing the Constituent Assembly? Listen to Trotsky:

"'Of course, the Constituent Assembly will have to be dispersed,' said Lenin, 'but what about the Left Socialist-Revolutionaries?'

"But our apprehensions were greatly allayed by old Natanson. He came in to 'take counsel' with us, and after the first few words he said:

"'We shall probably have to disperse the Constituent Assembly by force.'

"'Bravo!' exclaimed Lenin. 'What is true is true! But will your people agree to it?'

"'Some of our people are wavering, but I think that in the end they will agree,' answered Natanson."

That is how history is written.

Do you want to know how the Party settled the question about the Supreme Military Council? Listen to Trotsky:

"'Unless we have serious and experienced military experts we shall never extricate ourselves from this chaos,' I said to Vladimir Ilyich after every visit to the Staff.

"'That is evidently true, but they might betray us....'

"'Let us attach a commissar to each of them.'

"'Two would be better," exclaimed Lenin, 'and strong-handed ones. There surely must be strong-handed Communists in our ranks.'

"That is how the structure of the

Supreme Military Council arose."

That is how Trotsky writes history.

Why did Trotsky need these "Arabian Nights" stories derogatory to Lenin? Was it to exalt V. I. Lenin, the leader of the Party? It doesn't look like it.

The Party knows that Lenin was the greatest Marxist of our times, a profound theoretician and a most experienced revolutionary, to whom any trace of Blanquism was alien. Trotsky touches upon this aspect, too, in his book. But the portrait he paints is not that of the giant Lenin, but of a dwarf-like Blanquist who, in the October days, advises the Party "to take power by its own hand, independently of and behind the back of the Soviet." I have already said, however, that there is not a scrap of truth in this description.

Why did Trotsky need this flagrant ... inaccuracy? Is this not an attempt to discredit Lenin "just a little"?

Such are the characteristic features of the new Trotskyism.

What is the danger of this new Trotskyism? It is that Trotskyism, owing to its entire inner content, stands every chance of becoming the centre and rallying point of the non-proletarian elements who are striving to weaken, to disintegrate the proletarian dictatorship.

You will ask: what is to be done now? What are the Party's immediate tasks in connection with Trotsky's new literary pronouncements?

Trotskyism is taking action now in order to discredit Bolshevism and to undermine its foundations. It is the duty of the Party *to bury Trotskyism as an ideological trend.*

There is talk about repressive measures against the opposition and about the possibility of a split. That is nonsense, comrades. Our Party is strong and mighty. It will not allow any splits. As regards repressive measures, I am emphatically opposed to them. What we need now is not repressive measures, but an extensive ideological struggle against renascent Trotskyism.

We did not want and did not strive for this literary discussion. Trotskyism is forcing it upon us by its anti-Leninist pronouncements. Well, we are ready, comrades.